P9-BBV-590

DNA, GENES, AND CHROMOSOMES

by Mason Anders

CAPSTONE PRESS
a capstone imprint

Fact Finders Books are published by Capstone Press,
1710 Roe Crest Drive, North Mankato, Minnesota 56003
www.mycapstone.com

Copyright © 2018 by Capstone Press, a Capstone imprint. All rights reserved. No part of this publication may be reproduced in whole or in part, or stored in a retrieval system, or transmitted in any form or by any means, electronic, mechanical, photocopying, recording, or otherwise, without written permission of the publisher.

Library of Congress Cataloging-in-Publication Data
Names: Anders, Mason, author.
Title: DNA, genes, and chromosomes / by Mason Anders.
Description: North Mankato, Minnesota : Capstone Press, [2017] | Series: Fact finders. Genetics |
   Includes bibliographical references and index.
Identifiers: LCCN 2016055790
   ISBN 978-1-5157-7256-9 (library binding)
   ISBN 978-1-5157-7260-6 (paperback)
   ISBN 978-1-5157-7264-4 (ebook pdf)
Subjects: LCSH: DNA—Juvenile literature. | Genes—Juvenile literature. | Heredity—Juvenile literature.
   | Genetic disorders—Juvenile literature.
Classification: LCC QP624 .A54 2017 | DDC 572.8/6—dc23
LC record available at https://lccn.loc.gov/2016055790

Editorial Credits
Editor: Nikki Potts
Designer: Philippa Jenkins
Media Researcher: Morgan Walters and Jo Miller
Production Specialist: Katy LaVigne

Photo Credits
Shutterstock: alanto, cover (bottom), Designua, 23, 28, ellepigrafica, 10, 13, Festa, 11, Halfbottle, 19, Jezper, 25, joshya, 15, Kateryna Kon, cover (top), 3, 29, koya979, 21, Lebendkulturen.de, 14, Macrovector, 8, Mila Supinskaya Glashchenko, 6, Monkey Business Images, 16, Nata-Lia, 5, Sebastian Kaulitzki, 1, 27, special for you, throughout, (background), Valdis Skudre, 7, Zuzanae, 26

Printed and bound in China.
004640

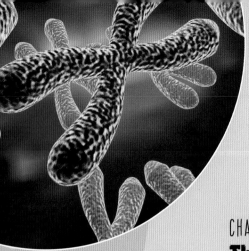

TABLE OF CONTENTS

CHAPTER 1
The Instruction Manual for Life....4

CHAPTER 2
DNA 8

CHAPTER 3
Genes 14

CHAPTER 4
Chromosomes 20

CHAPTER 5
Diseases and Disorders............... 26

Glossary 30

Read More 31

Internet Sites 31

Critical Thinking Questions............. 32

Index 32

The Instruction Manual for Life

If you have ever built a model airplane, you probably followed an instruction manual. It told you what parts you needed to use and how to put them together.

Your body, as well as every living thing, also has an instruction manual. It is a collection of long, stringy molecules called deoxyribonucleic acid, or DNA. Most of our bodies' cells contain about 6 feet (2 meters) of DNA. In plants and animals, DNA is in a part of the cell called the nucleus.

DNA has a shape called a double helix. It looks like a twisted ladder.

Like most instruction manuals, DNA is divided into sections. Each DNA strand contains thousands of sections. These sections, called genes, are the basic units of **heredity**. Each gene tells the cell how to make a specific **protein**.

> **Inherited** genes determine traits such as hair and eye color.

heredity—the process of passing physical and mental qualities from a parent to a child before the child is born

protein—chemical made by plant and animal cells to carry out various functions

inherit—to receive a characteristic from a parent

Genes determine all of an animal's characteristics. In a giraffe, that would include spots and long necks.

Genes direct how living things grow, work, and reproduce. Birds have wings and giraffes have long necks because of their genes. Genes determine your hair color and the shape of your nose. One cell's complete set of genes is called a genome.

DNA is packaged into structures called **chromosomes**. Humans have 23 pairs of chromosomes. One set from each pair comes from the mother. The other set comes from the father. We are a blend of the traits we've inherited from our parents.

chromosome—threadlike structure in the nucleus that carries the genes

CHAPTER 2

DNA

To understand the DNA instruction manual, it helps to know the language of the genome. It is written in a genetic code. That code is made up of four chemicals. We call these chemicals **bases**. They are adenine, thymine, cytosine, and guanine. Scientists call them A, T, C, and G for short.

FACT

Thymine and cytosine are called pyrimidines. They are single-ring nitrogenous bases. Adenine and guanine are called purines. They are double-ring nitrogenous bases.

Thymine always pairs with adenine. Guanine always pairs with cytosine.

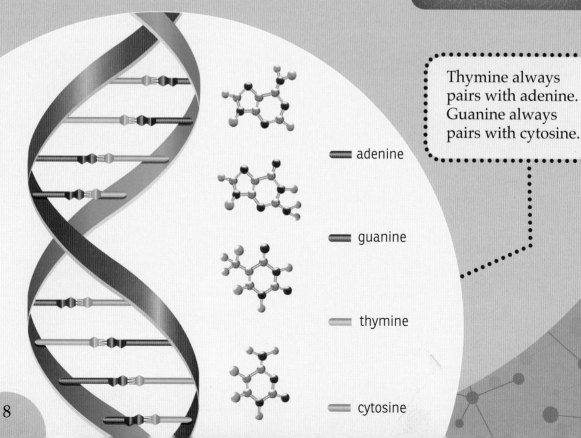

adenine

guanine

thymine

cytosine

The long, twisted ladder of DNA is made up of bases. Any one of the four bases is lined up on the long sides of the ladder. Two bases join in the middle to form the rungs.

If you were to look at one of the strands of a DNA molecule, you might see a section that looks like this:

ATTCAGGGTCTAATGATCGTGTGA

Cells read the string of letters in groups of three-letter words, or **codons**.

ATT CAG GGT CTA ATG ATC GTG TGA

The body uses 20 different building blocks to make proteins. Each codon tells the cell to use a specific building block. Thousands of codons make a gene. Each gene tells the cell how to make a specific protein. The sequence "TGA" means stop. It tells the cell to stop making the protein.

WHAT DO PROTEINS DO?

We usually think of protein as being a kind of food. Meat and tofu are good sources of protein. But our bodies make their own proteins. These proteins do the work of the cell. They help the heart beat. They help intestines digest food. They relay messages within the body. Our body tissues and organs are made of proteins.

Proteins called **enzymes** make certain chemical reactions possible. Hormones are proteins that direct many body functions. They help you develop and grow. They tell you when you are hungry or thirsty. They let you know when you are cold.

Unzipping the Ladder

DNA can be "unzipped" down the middle of its two-part rungs. There are two important reasons for DNA to unzip.

First, DNA unzips to make an exact copy of itself. Living things grow because their cells divide and multiply. Our bodies make new cells to replace old or damaged cells. Each new cell needs a DNA copy. Each unzipped strand becomes a guide for forming a matching strand.

The second reason a DNA ladder unzips is so that the cell can make proteins. Only the section of DNA containing the gene for that protein unzips.

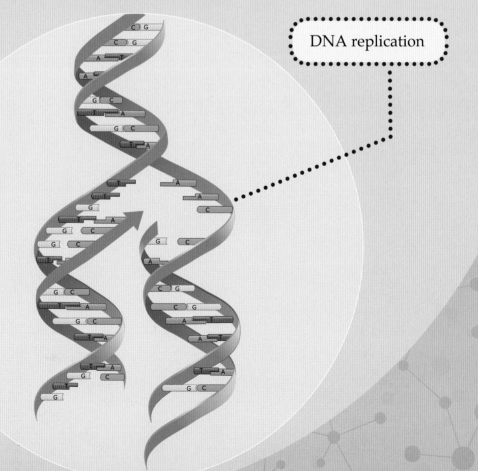

DNA replication

Changes in DNA

A mutation is a change in the order of bases on a strand of DNA. Cells use an enzyme to copy their DNA before dividing. After a cell divides, each new cell normally has a full copy of the genome. But sometimes the enzyme makes a mistake. It may switch one base for another. It may leave out a base. It may insert an extra base.

These mistakes are common. The cell usually catches these mistakes. It repairs them as it goes along. If the mistakes are not repaired, genes will produce proteins that are different or damaged.

FACT

Outside factors in the environment can cause the enzyme to make more mistakes. These factors are called mutagens. Sunlight and X-rays can cause mutations. Chemicals found in cigarette smoke are also powerful mutagens. Mutations sometimes happen after we become infected with a virus or bacteria. However, scientists do not yet know all of the things that can cause mutations.

damaged DNA strand

Types of Mutations

Imagine the original DNA strand looks like this:

TAG CTC CGA GTC

Deletion

During deletion one or more bases are deleted. In the example, the second G base has been deleted. This causes the rest of the DNA code to be read differently. This may cause the wrong building blocks to be placed in a protein.

TAG CTC CAG TC

Inversion

During inversion the order of the bases is reversed. Only a section of the code is affected. In this section, the wrong building blocks are put into a protein. The remaining DNA code is not changed.

TAG CTC AGC GTC

Substitution

One base replaces another during substitution. A different building block may be inserted in the protein. In the example, a T base replaces a C base, which results in TGA. This is the stop codon. The enzyme will stop working, even if it is in the middle of making the protein. The protein will not be complete.

TAG CTC TGA GTC

Insertion

One or more bases are added during insertion. In the example, an A base was inserted into the beginning of the third codon. Like deletion, this affects all of the remaining DNA code. It causes the rest of the code to be read differently. Again, the wrong building blocks may be assembled into a protein.

TAG CTC ACG AGT C

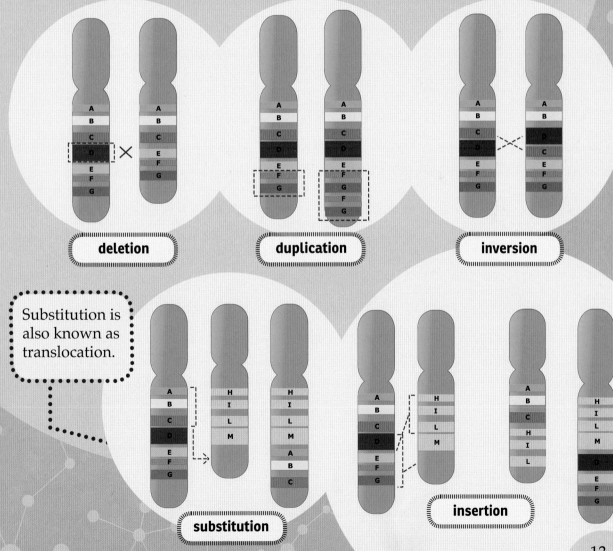

Substitution is also known as translocation.

deletion

duplication

inversion

substitution

insertion

CHAPTER 3

Genes

Living things have hundreds to tens of thousands of genes in their genome. Bread yeast cells have 5,770 genes. Humans have an estimated 20,000 to 25,000 genes.

Each cell in an organism contains a complete set of that organism's genes. However, not all of the genes are active in every cell. In a muscle cell, only the genes for muscle cells are turned on. In a plant leaf cell, only the genes for leaf cells are turned on.

FACT

The animal with the most genes is the water flea, *Daphnia pulex*. Although almost microscopic, it has about 31,000 genes.

water flea

Where Do Genes Come From?

Children inherit their genes from their parents. Half of the child's genes come from the mother. Half come from the father.

Genes found on chromosomes determine what traits children will have.

eye color

blood type

hair color

growth

If we get all our chromosomes from our parents, why don't we look exactly like them? Family members often do resemble each other in many ways. But sometimes they look very different. Your mother and father may both have dark hair. Your hair might be light brown or red. This happens because the gene that determines hair color has several forms. These forms are called **alleles**.

A baby with dark hair has inherited either one or two alleles for dark hair from his or her parents.

You inherit one allele for each gene from your father and one from your mother. These alleles get mixed up during reproduction. They can combine in a number of new ways. These new combinations produce a unique person.

When a mother and father do not have the same type of alleles, the baby gets a mixture of alleles. A father may have alleles for blond hair, while the mother has black-haired alleles. What hair color will the baby have? It depends on which alleles are **dominant**.

Babies inherit alleles for every kind of trait. Some alleles are dominant. Others are **recessive**. The alleles for black hair are dominant. Those for blond hair are recessive. If a baby receives two alleles for black hair, he or she will have black hair. If another child receives two alleles for blond hair, he or she will have blond hair. A baby with one allele for black hair and one for blond hair will most likely have black hair because the black hair allele is dominant.

MUTATIONS AND ALLELES

Alleles are caused by mutations. Most mutations are neither good nor bad. There are sections of DNA in between genes that do not seem to code for any protein. Mutations that happen in these areas often have no effect at all. Most often, mutations simply give rise to variations that make every human unique. They may cause freckles or differently colored eyes.

Some mutations have a positive effect. They lead to new versions of proteins that help individuals adapt to their environment. Individuals with those helpful variations pass their genes on to the next generation.

dominant—the form of a gene most likely to produce a trait in offspring
recessive—the form of a gene most likely to stay hidden

Is My Genome Unique?

Some people are tall. Others are short. Some people have dark skin. Others are pale. However, we're all very similar at the DNA level. The genomes of any two people differ by less than 1 percent. Chimpanzees share 98 percent of our human genes. Even fruit flies have their own version of 44 percent of our genes. Many of these shared genes are necessary for basic cell function.

Our shared DNA shows how we are related to other living things. But those tiny differences in our genomes make us unique as individuals and as humans. Even identical twins are unique. Identical twins occur when a single fertilized egg divides into two cells. These cells develop into two separate **embryos**. They have the same genetic makeup, but as their cells divide and multiply, mutations sometimes occur. The genomes of the newborn twins are likely to have hundreds of mutations.

embryo—an animal organism in its early stages of development

While identical twins share many similar traits, their genomes differ.

CHAPTER 4

Chromosomes

The human genome is long. The DNA from a single cell, stretched out into a single thread, would be about 6 feet (2 meters) long. Without some kind of packaging system, these long, thin DNA molecules would never fit inside the **nucleus**.

DNA molecules are wrapped around proteins. These proteins are called histones. Together, they are like spools of thread. These spools are called **nucleosomes**.

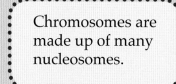

Chromosomes are made up of many nucleosomes.

nucleus—command center of the cell that gives instructions to the other parts of the cell

nucleosome—repeating units of chromatin that consist of a complex of DNA and histone

When it is time for the cell to divide, the nucleosomes line up. They are like beads on a string. They become a chromatin fiber. The fiber loops and coils again to make a chromosome.

We can see chromosomes under the microscope. Each chromosome has two short arms and two long arms. They are joined at the center by a **centromere**, creating an X shape.

At the end of each chromosome is a repeating sequence of DNA called a **telomere**. Telomeres protect the ends of chromosomes. They are like the plastic tips on shoelaces. In many types of cells, telomeres lose a bit of their DNA every time the cell divides. When all of the telomere DNA is gone, the cell cannot copy itself, and it dies.

During cell division, it is important that every DNA molecule is copied. They must all be evenly split up between the cells. Chromosomes are a key part of that process.

centromere—point on a chromosome where the spindle, protein fibers, attaches during cell division

telomere—the natural end of a chromosome

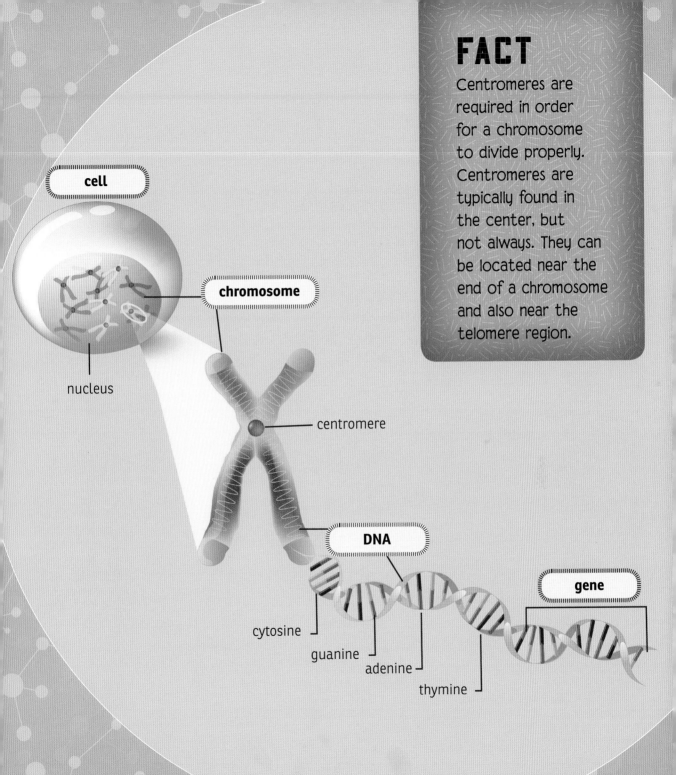

cell

nucleus

chromosome

FACT

Centromeres are required in order for a chromosome to divide properly. Centromeres are typically found in the center, but not always. They can be located near the end of a chromosome and also near the telomere region.

centromere

DNA

gene

cytosine

guanine

adenine

thymine

23

Living Things

All living things have chromosomes. They vary in number and shape. Most bacteria have just one or two chromosomes. They are shaped like circles. Dogs have 78 chromosomes. Human body cells have 23 pairs of stick-shaped chromosomes, equaling 46 in total.

Human sex cells have just 23 chromosomes. Each egg or sperm cell contains a sex chromosome. There are two sex chromosomes. They are called X and Y. Eggs carry only X chromosomes. Sperm carry either an X or Y chromosome. Sperm and egg cells unite during reproduction. The result is a fertilized egg. This fertilized egg now contains the full set of 46 chromosomes. A girl inherits two X chromosomes, one from each of her parents. A boy gets an X chromosome from his mother and a Y chromosome from his father.

Sperm and egg unite during reproduction to create a fertilized egg that has a full set of chromosomes.

Diseases and Disorders

Chromosomes

Changes in the number or structure of chromosomes may lead to serious problems. Chromosome changes happen in about 1 out of 150 babies born.

Children born with Down syndrome have an extra chromosome. This causes mental disabilities and other physical challenges. A girl born with only one sex chromosome, an X, will have Turner syndrome. Girls with Turner syndrome are very short. Most do not go through puberty unless they receive hormones.

Down syndrome trisomy 21 occurs when there are three instances of a chromosome instead of two.

Parts of chromosomes may be missing or duplicated. A portion of one chromosome might be transferred to another chromosome. Part of the chromosome might break off, turn upside down, and reattach. A piece of the chromosome might even break off and form a ring. Some types of cancer are the result of a chromosome made up of joined pieces of broken chromosomes.

illustration of a magnified cancer cell

Mutations

Cells divide and multiply as the body grows. The body makes new cells to replace dead or damaged cells. Mutations in the genes that control cell division can cause cells to grow out of control. They develop strange sizes and shapes. They destroy healthy cells. They may form lumps of tissues called tumors. They can take over blood cells. These types of mutations are one of the main causes of cancer. Tumors can prevent organs from working as well as they should.

One example occurs when tumors destroy healthy tissue in the lungs. The lungs cannot do a good job of bringing oxygen into the body. Cancer cells can also travel throughout the body. They create new tumors that damage and destroy tissues in other organs.

Inherited Diseases

Some diseases are caused by inherited mutations. These types of mutations are passed from parent to child. Sickle cell anemia is caused by a defect in the gene that codes for a protein in red blood cells. This protein carries oxygen through the bloodstream.

Red blood cells are usually flat and round. The defective protein causes the red blood cells to be shaped like a sickle instead. A sickle is a cutting tool shaped like a crescent moon. These sickle-shaped cells can block small blood vessels. They prevent oxygen from reaching the tissues. This blockage can be very painful. It can even lead to death.

Hemoglobin is the protein in blood cells that carries oxygen.

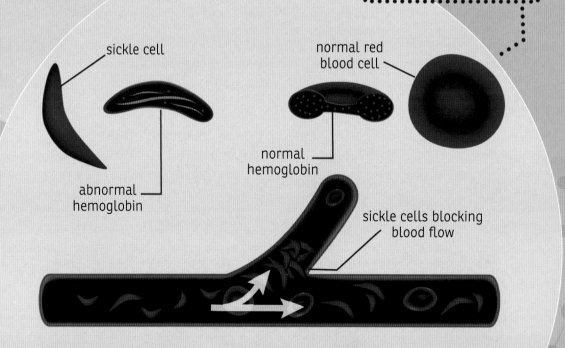

sickle cell

abnormal hemoglobin

normal red blood cell

normal hemoglobin

sickle cells blocking blood flow

A person who inherits just one copy of the defective gene will have a mild form of the disease. He or she is a carrier of the trait. People who have inherited two copies of the defective gene have a much more severe disease.

SICKLE CELL ANEMIA

In some parts of Africa, the sickle cell mutation is very common. Up to 40 percent of Africans carry at least one defective gene. How could such a harmful defect become so common?

The sickle cell gene is especially common in areas hard-hit by malaria. Malaria is a disease that kills more than 1 million people every year. It is transferred to humans through mosquito bites.

Carriers of the trait have some resistance to malaria. Their red blood cells become sickle-shaped when they are infected with the malaria parasite. Their bodies remove the infected cells because of the sickle shape. They get rid of the parasite along with the cells.

In areas where malaria is common, having one sickle cell gene is a good thing. Those carriers are more likely to survive malaria.

The African population is like a very large family. The sickle cell gene has survived because it allows many people to survive malaria infections.

Malaria parasites first infect liver cells and then red blood cells. The parasites grow inside and eventually destroy the cell.

Glossary

allele (UH-leel)—one of two genes in a pair contributed by a parent

base (BASE)—one of four basic chemicals that form the rungs of the DNA ladder

centromere (sen-TROH-meer)—point on a chromosome where the spindle, protein fibers, attaches during cell division

chromosome (KROH-muh-sohm)—threadlike structure in the nucleus that carries the genes

codon (CO-duhn)—a three-base unit of genetic code

dominant (DAH-muh-nuhnt)—the form of a gene most likely to produce a trait in offspring

embryo (EM-bree-oh)—an animal organism in its early stages of development

enzyme (EN-zime)—a protein that helps break down food

heredity (huh-RED-i-tee)—the process of passing physical and mental qualities from a parent to a child before the child is born

inherit (in-HER-it)—to receive a characteristic from a parent

nucleosome (NYOO-klee-oh-suhm)—repeating units of chromatin that consist of a complex of DNA and histone

nucleus (NYOO-klee-uhss)—command center of the cell that gives instructions to the other parts of the cell

protein (PROH-teen)—chemical made by plant and animal cells to carry out various functions

recessive (REE-ses-ive)—the form of a gene most likely to stay hidden

telomere (TEE-lo-meer)—the natural end of a chromosome

Read More

Albright, R. N. *The Double Helix Structure of DNA: James Watson, Francis Crick, Maurice Wilkins, and Rosalind Franklin.* Revolutionary Discoveries of Scientific Pioneers. New York: The Rosen Publishing Group, Inc., 2014.

Ballen, Karen Gunnison. *Decoding Our DNA: Craig Venter vs. Human Genome Project.* Scientific Rivalries and Scandals. Minneapolis: Twenty-First Century Books, 2013.

Nelson, Maria. *Cells Up Close*. Under the Microscope. New York: Gareth Stevens Publishing, 2014.

Internet Sites

FactHound offers a safe, fun way to find Internet sites related to this book. All of the sites on FactHound have been researched by our staff.

Here's all you do:

Visit *www.facthound.com*

Type in this code: 9781515772569

Super-cool stuff! Check out projects, games and lots more at **www.capstonekids.com**

Critical Thinking Questions

- DNA strands are composed of thousands of sections. What are these sections called?

- What are some effects of gene mutation?

- Take a look at the diagram on page 13. What type of mutation occurs when a base is reversed?

Index

alleles, 16, 17

bases, 8, 9, 11, 12, 13

centromeres, 22, 23

Down syndrome, 26

enzymes, 9, 11, 12

genomes, 7, 8, 11, 14, 18, 20

histones, 20

malaria, 29
mutagens, 11
mutations, 11, 12–13, 17, 18, 27, 28, 29

nucleosomes, 20, 22
nucleus, 4, 20

purines, 8
pyrimidines, 8

sickle cell anemia, 28, 29

telomeres, 22, 23
tumors, 27
Turner syndrome, 26